Book Trailer Boot Camp
A Step By Step Guide

Heart of Jupiter Publishing

ISBN-13:978-0692280676 (Heart of Jupiter Publishing)

ISBN-10:0692280677

Cover

© Alanpoulson | Dreamstime.com - Woman Leg In Boots On Books Photo

Design: Heart of Jupiter Publishing

Susan Ann Wall is a multi-genre, multi-published author of contemporary romance, women's fiction and erotic fiction (you can find her erotic titles under the pseudonym Ann Victor). Many of her story ideas come from real life adventures, like being trapped at her desk by a sinister wolf spider or randomly running into her gynecologist on an airplane.

A U.S. Army veteran, Susan traveled extensively before settling in her hometown in the majestic White Mountains of New Hampshire. She's passionate about all things purple, Bon Jovi, dark chocolate, and tea. When she's not tapping away on her purple netbook, she enjoys skiing and kayaking with her three kids and drinking a nice cold one with her Hero Husband (after all, he does rescue her from those sinister wolf spiders).

Susan is Microsoft Office Specialist Master certified, holds a Master of Arts in Education in Curriculum and Instruction and a Bachelor of Arts in English and Communication Arts. She has made a living for many years as an instructor and instructional designer. She has taught Microsoft courses for organizations large and small including Lockheed Martin, the National Security Agency, Green Mountain Coffee Roasters, CompUSA, the U.S. Navy, and to small business owners through White Mountains Community College. Susan has also taught and shared marketing techniques to small business owners through workshops and personalized consulting. Additionally, Susan has presented workshops to the New Hampshire Romance Writers of America chapter, the Women's Rural Entrepreneurial Network, and at New Hampshire Writer's Project Writer's Day and New Jersey Romance Writers Put Your Heart in a Book conference. Visit her website for a full list of available workshops and available books.

Susan is a member of NHRWA, RWA-WF, NH Writers' Project, New England Independent Writers, Book Boyfriend Café, and RomVets.

e-mail: susan@susanannwall.com

susanannwall.com

annvictor.com

Find Author **Susan Ann Wall** and **Ann Victor** on Facebook and Twitter.

Introduction

Watch the following trailers or trailers of your choosing and make notes of your observations about the media used, theme, etc.

Trailer #1 Observations (Business Trip)

Trailer #2 Observations (Quitting the Boss)

Trailer #3 Observations (The Sound of Betrayal)

Why PowerPoint?

If you've seen PowerPoint presentations, you're probably used to bullet point lists, but that's just a very small part of what PowerPoint can do. It's actually an incredibly powerful program ... unfortunately most people don't use it to its fullest potential. The intent of this step-by-step guide is to change how you look at and use PowerPoint. It can be a very powerful tool for marketing and one of those marketing tools is book trailers.

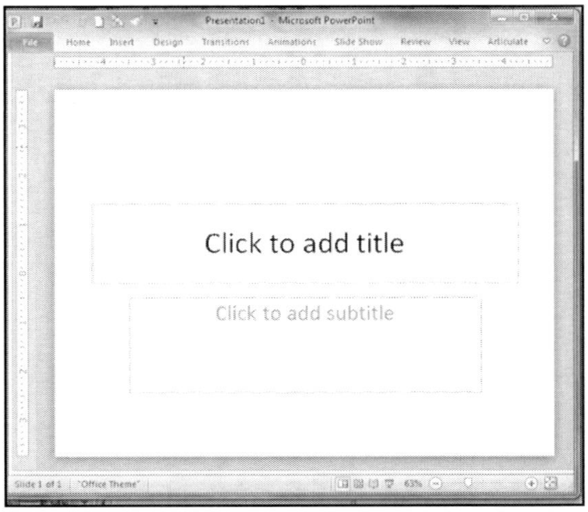

If you watched the video examples on the previous page, you may be stunned that each of them were created in PowerPoint. Instead of thinking of PowerPoint in terms of death by bullets, think of it as a blank canvas. On a blank canvas, your only limitation is your imagination.

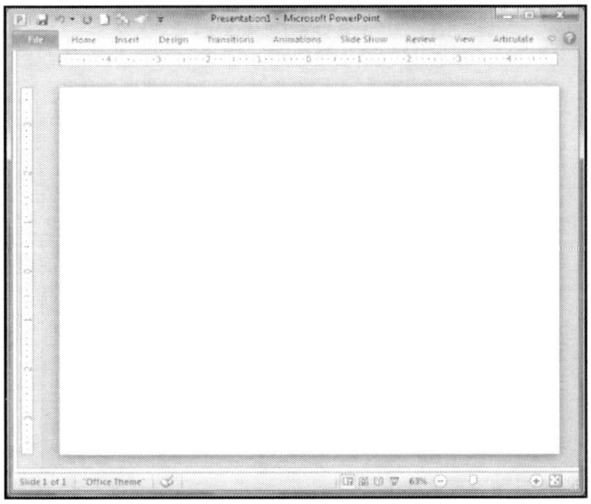

Media

Media elements play an important role in your trailer. You can include images, audio, and video. You want to choose media that represents elements of your story or the message you are trying to communicate with your trailer.

One of the important things to consider with media use is having permissions or the right to use images. If the media belongs to you, for example, a picture that you took, you're covered, but even with clip art images in the MS Office gallery, you need to read the terms of use to ensure you aren't violating the terms of use policy. Generally speaking, if you are not selling the video or requiring payment for people to view it, then you are covered under the usage terms.

There are plenty of sites that offer free stock images, music, and videos, or for a small fee. Again, be sure to read the terms of use.

If you are using media provided by a friend or someone else who has copyright, you may want to consider using a release. You can find generic release agreements by doing an internet search. Have the person providing the image sign the release and retain a copy of the agreement.

Images

A picture speaks a thousand words, so it is likely you will want to use images in your trailer. You're likely going to have your cover image in the video, and you may use other images to represent other elements of the story.

The first question you'll need to answer is *will you use images*? You have many different options for using images, including those listed here:

- Cover art, full or cropped
- Images to create cover art
- Images that relate to the story

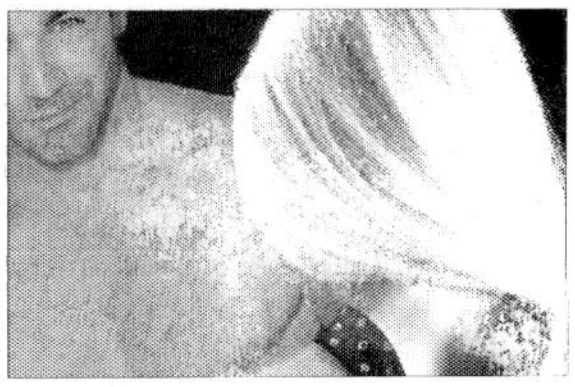

(Male Image: © Curaphotography | Dreamstime.com)
(Female Image: © Branislav Ostojic | Dreamstime.com)
Cover Art Design: Heart of Jupiter Publishing

Finding Images

There are countless places to find images. Obviously, if you have access to the image(s) used to create your cover art, or even simply the cover art itself, then you may not need to search for additional images. Your image needs will depend on the design of your trailer, availability of images that meet your design, and your budget.

If the image is one that you've taken, you're covered, but even with clip art images in the MS Office gallery, you need to read the terms of use to ensure you aren't violence the policy. Generally speaking, if you are not selling the video or requiring payment for people to view it, then you are probably covered.

There are plenty of sites that offer free stock images or stock images for a fee ... again, be sure to read the terms of use.

If you are using an image provided by a friend or someone else who has copyright, you may want to consider using a release. You can find generic release agreements by doing an internet search. Have the person providing the image sign the release and retain a copy of the agreement.

Examples of where to find images:

- Stock photo images – some are free, some are not. A few examples of stock image sites include:
  - Wylio.com
  - Dreamstime.com
  - Google search: free stock photos
- Microsoft Gallery: Microsoft terms and conditions: File -> Help -> Microsoft Software License Terms -> Section C.

  ALWAYS READ THE TERMS OF USE!

- Personal Images
  - Landscapes, Cityscapes, Landmarks, Furniture, Pets, Car, Collectibles, etc. (Seattle Image: © Susan Ann Wall)
- Images from Friends
  - If friends have images they are willing to let you use, be sure to have them sign a photo release. See Appendix A for a sample Standard Photo Release.

Using Images

You may have an image or images in mind when you design your trailer or you may design the trailer around the available images. Once you have those images, in considering your design, you will need to determine how to use the images. Remember that a PowerPoint slide functions like a blank canvas. You can do anything you want with it. You have several creative options:

- Background
- Foreground
- Full screen
- Pieces
- Layering

(Image of Couple:© Nikita Buida | Dreamstime.com)
(Boston and Seattle Images: © Susan Ann Wall)

Image Effects

Once your image or images are selected, there are a variety of formatting effects you can apply in PowerPoint. The effects you choose will need to work with other design elements on your slide, including text and background color.

- Flip
- Crop
- Angle
- Color
- Remove background
- Soft edges
- Border

© Konradbak | Dreamstime.com

Let's look at an example of how these effects were used in the *When the Boss Gets Jealous* trailer.

On the left, you can see the original image, but in the video as shown below, you can see I've used a variety of techniques on the photo.

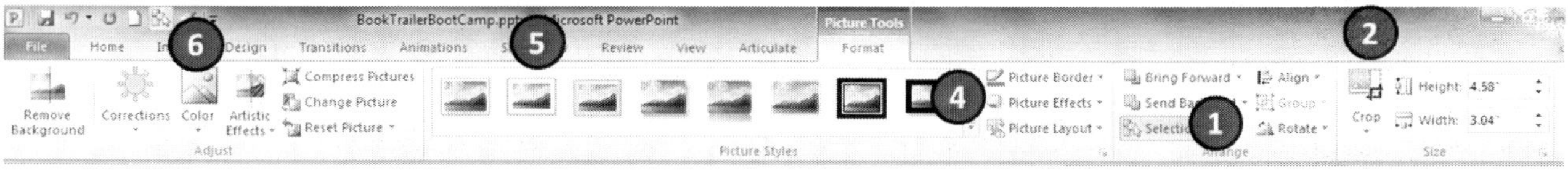

1. First, I've flipped the image horizontally. On the Format ribbon, use the Rotate option.
2. I've also cropped the image so that I'm only using a portion of it on this slide. With the image selected, use the Crop option on the Format ribbon. Left click and drag the handles around the image.
3. Next, I changed the angle of the image using the rotate handle that is on the image (green handle at top of image).

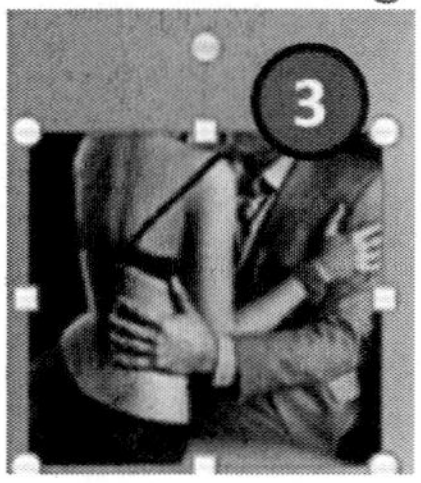

4. Then I added a soft edge which is what creates that blurry edge. The soft edge option is found under the Picture Effects menu on the format ribbon bar.
5. In the lower left corner, there's a black and white snapshot of the image. To get this effect, I used the Picture Styles option that created the white border
6. Then I used the Color option to change it to grayscale. Again, I adjusted the angle using the rotate handle on the image.

Another option that is really useful is the Remove Background option.

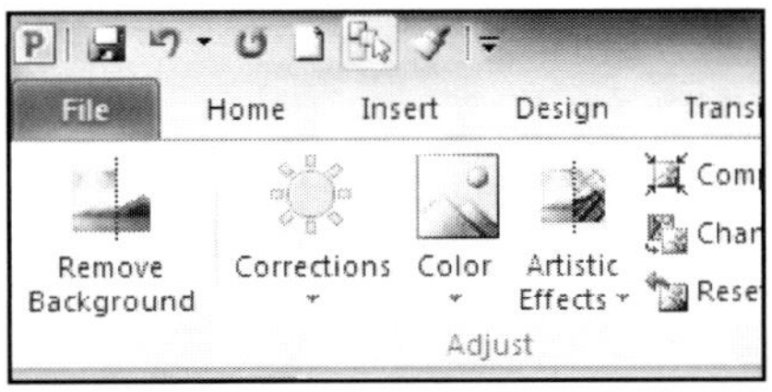

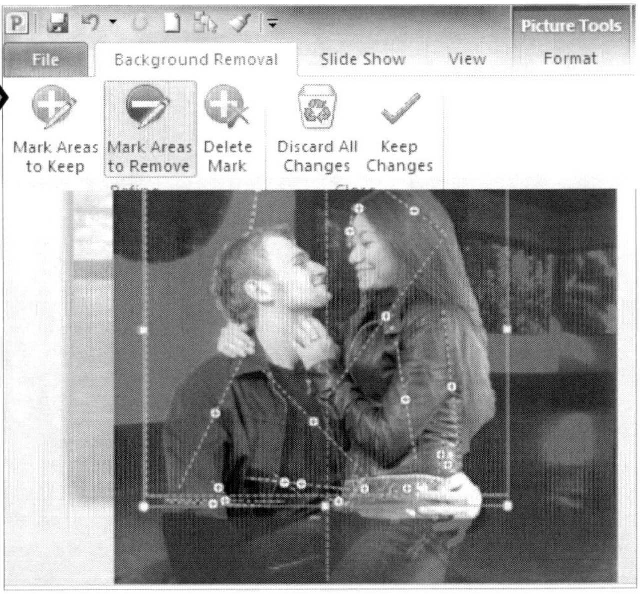

© Nikita Buida | Dreamstime.com

With the picture selected, click the Remove Background option on the Format ribbon. The Background Removal menu will open and there will be a square around your picture with much of the image shown in purple. The purple is what will be hidden when you select Keep Changes.

You can resize the box around the image to limit or increase the editable area. Then you will use the **Mark Areas to Keep** option to draw lines on the areas you want to keep (only if they turn purple). Use the **Mark Areas to Remove** option to draw lines on areas you want removed. This is a finicky tool and areas will change color as you continue to mark, so be patient.

When you are satisfied with the edits, click the **Keep Changes** button.

Audio

You probably don't want to leave your viewers hanging with a video that is completely silent, but at the same time, you don't want to overwhelm them with too much audio. You have a few different options for audio ... you can use music, do voice overs, or add sound effects. When you are designing your video, think about what would work best for your trailer.

As with all media, again, be sure to read the terms of use.

To insert a file, open the Insert ribbon and in the Audio drop down menu, select **Audio from file...**, choose your file, and voila. It will appear as a speaker icon on your slide and there are lots of different options you have. You can have the music start automatically, have it play on a single slide or across multiple slides, you can even edit where the music starts and/or stops using the PowerPoint tools. These options are outlined later in this book.

© Yuri_arcurs | Dreamstime.com

Using Music

If you decide to use music in your trailer, there are different options available.

- **Free stock music**: Follow the terms of use! You can find free stock music by doing an Internet search. One useful website to find free stock music is www.freestockmusic.com. You can also purchase an entire album of full-length trailer music for about the same cost as a music CD at www.icontrailermusic.com.
- **Bands you know**: If you know an indie band, you may be able to use their music and do some cross promotion! Be sure to have the band members sign a release for you to use the music and ensure they own the rights.

Things to consider with music:

- **Format**: There are many different formats of audio files, including mp3, m4a, wav, wma, etc. PowerPoint accepts many different file types, so you just need to ensure the file you plan to use is in an accepted format. If it is not, there are digital conversation software tools available for free or at minimal cost.
- **Length**: You will need to decide if you want the audio file to play for just want slide, for a specific period of time, or for the entire trailer. The audio clip may be too long for your purposes, so you may need to trim it down. You can trim the audio in PowerPoint or you can use a free audio editing program such as Audacity to trim the audio.

Voice Over Narration?

Another audio option is voice overs. To do voice overs, you need to have a decent (not necessarily expensive) microphone and audio recording software such as Audacity (or you can record directly in PowerPoint).

I recommend creating one audio clip per slide and have your script written so you aren't recording off the cuff. If you have a willing friend, you could use someone else's voice instead of your own or you could use more than one … female POV, male POV, or maybe a fun conversation between two friends.

To record using PowerPoint, from the Insert ribbon, open the Audio menu and select Record Audio. A Record Sound dialogue box will open. Name the recording, hit the record button, and talk into the microphone. When you are finished, press the Stop button. The recording will insert onto the slide and you'll be able to edit and format it as you would any other audio clip you insert. We'll look at formatting options later in the book.

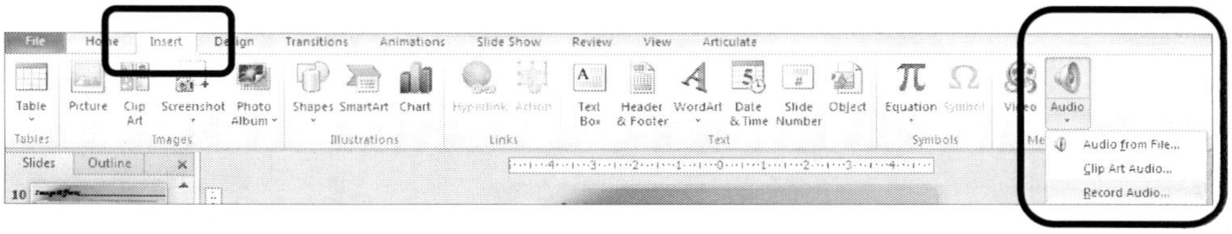

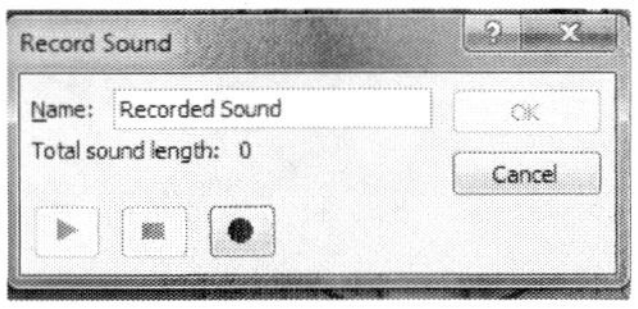

Sound Effects

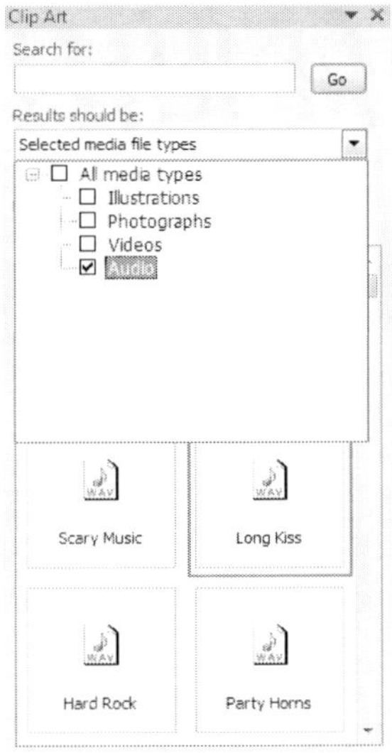

The MS Gallery has a limited number of sound effects that you can search on in the clip art gallery. Just remember, you are trying to entice people to read your books, not annoy them with obnoxious sounds. Make sure if you decide to use sound effects clip, it works with your trailer.

To insert an audio clip from the MS Gallery, open the Insert ribbon and select Clip Art. You can search on keywords, but ensure you have Audio selected from the media file types.

Video

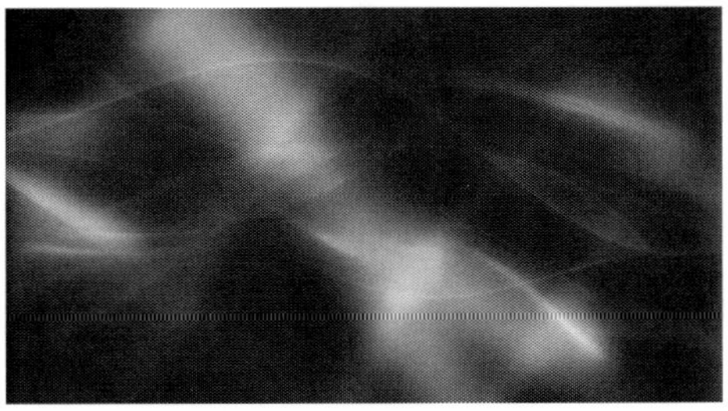

www.motionbackgroundsforfree.com

You can insert video files into your trailer. You might be thinking, *I'm making a video, why would I need to insert video?* Well, the simple answer is maybe because an existing video clip would work with your trailer.

In the *Business Trip* book trailer, (the one with the hunky naked guy and the swirling colors in the background), the swirling colors are courtesy of a video clip used as the background.

As always, read the terms of use for any video clips you insert.

Finding Videos

There are plenty of websites where you can find free stock videos. Motionbackgroundsforfree.com and videoblocks.com are just a couple (videoblocks.com requires a subscription, but you can take advantage of their 7 day free trial).

If you have a video camera or know someone who does, you can also make your own clips to use. This makes your trailer a little more complicated to develop because you may have to edit the videos and make sure they are in the proper format to insert into PowerPoint (or if you have video editing skills you could simply make your trailer using video editing software). This book does not cover how to use video editing software or how to create your own video clip.

Using Videos

When deciding on a video, you'll need to consider its placement. You can have it take up the full screen or only part of the screen, depending on how it will support your trailer. If you are using full screen, you'll likely use it in the background and if it is partial screen, placement may be in the foreground. Then you'll have to decide on screen position, whether it's centered or to the side, whether you angle it, etc.

- Background
- Foreground
- Full screen
- Partial screen

In this example, a full motion background was extended to the full screen size. It is used as the background, with images and text layered on top of it.

Business Trip by Ann Victor book trailer

Text

Use of text can range from heavy to no use at all. It depends on the other elements in your video and how you intend to communicate your story. If you are using audio clips to reveal information about the story, you may not need text at all.

If you use music in your trailers, you may need to rely on text to convey the story. This can range from very brief to lengthy. It completely depends on the story and the design of the trailer. Text can be used for the title or tag line of your book, to introduce characters, or to tell the story. You can also choose between text boxes and word art.

When considering text, think about your font style. You may want to select a font style that compliments the cover art, particularly with short pieces of text, such as the book title or tag line. If you are using a significant amount of text, you want something that is easy to read. You also want a color that contrasts with the images so you can read it.

Concept

The possibilities are endless when you're developing a concept for your trailer.

You can use a trailer to create **intrigue**. You aren't necessarily revealing anything about your characters or the story, but you are creating interest for the reader. This is also a good way to introduce a series. The trailer simply includes short pieces of text that outline the rules for the resort where the story takes place, but it doesn't introduce the characters or the plots.

© Ricmcd | Dreamstime.com

You already have a **synopsis** of sorts…the back cover blurb. In this example, parts of the back cover blurb were used to reveal what the story is about.

© Yuri_arcurs | Dreamstime.com

You can also **have a character tell a story**. In Miranda Neville's trailer for *The Importance of Being Wicked*, Miranda's cat Ernie tells about the novel and what happens in it, from a cat's perspective, of course. It's a very clever way of creating a trailer if you don't have access to images that are relevant to your novel.

You can also **have a narrator tell a story**. Here, we find out a little information about Lyndsey Harper. This doesn't come from the book … it's just a little trivia about Lyndsey to create a rapport with the viewer … and then the story is revealed.

(c) Somakram | Dreamstime.com

What other concepts can you think of?

____

Branding

Your books are branded, right? They have your name. If you have a publisher, their logo appears somewhere. If you self-publish, you've come up with your own brand. You'll even see series that have some sort of brand. You will want to consider extending that brand to your trailers.

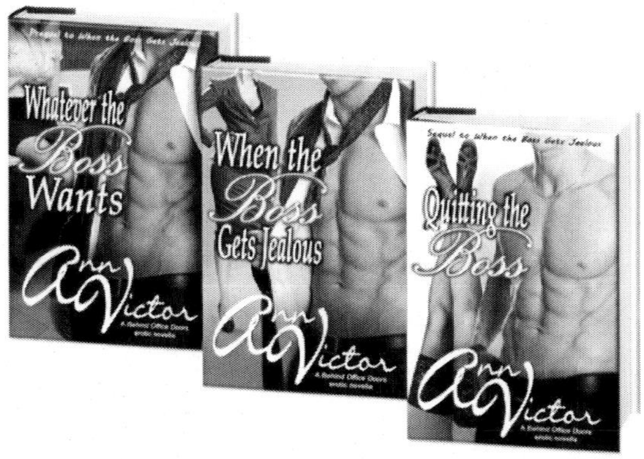

Your Name

Your name needs to appear in the trailer. Whether it's the last slide, somewhere in the middle or at the beginning will depend on your design and concept, but it's important to make it big and bold. You want readers to remember who wrote this book that they are now dying to read!!

Male image: (c) Dash | Dreamstime.com
Fmeale image: (c) Konradbak | Dreamstime.com

Your Website

You want your potential new readers to be able to find out more about you and your books. It's cumbersome to include all your social media sites, so keep it simple and send them directly to your website.

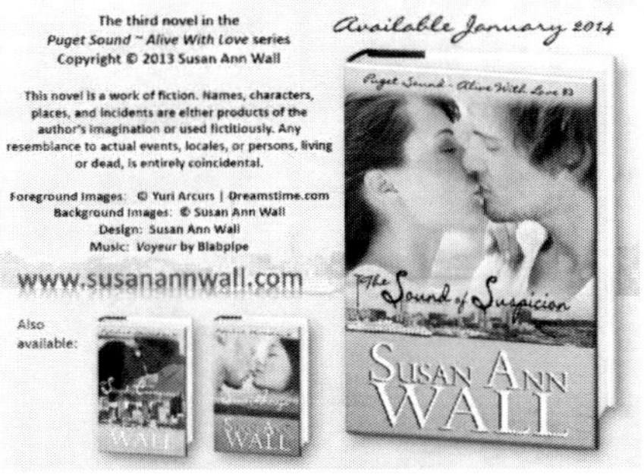

Book Cover

If you can, use your book cover in the trailer. Maybe you'll use it at the beginning, maybe at the end, but the purpose of the trailer is to sell the book, and readers will be able to find it more easily if they recognize it.

In this first example, not only do I put the book cover on the last slide, but I also put the previous three books in the series. Additionally, I use the images from the book cover throughout the trailer to increase that familiarity.

In the second example, I didn't use the book cover itself on the final slide, but I did use the cover art (note, this is from the original release – the book has since been rebranded with new cover art). As you can see, the images on the left are almost identical to the images on the cover. I will admit for this example, I changed the title font after the trailer was published, otherwise the same font would have appeared in the trailer as well.

PowerPoint Features

This section of the book provides step-by-step guidance on how to use some of the features in PowerPoint 2010 (and later versions) to create your trailer.

Change the Layout to Blank

1. From the Home ribbon, open the Layout menu.
2. Select Blank.

   Now when you insert a new slide, it will have the blank layout.

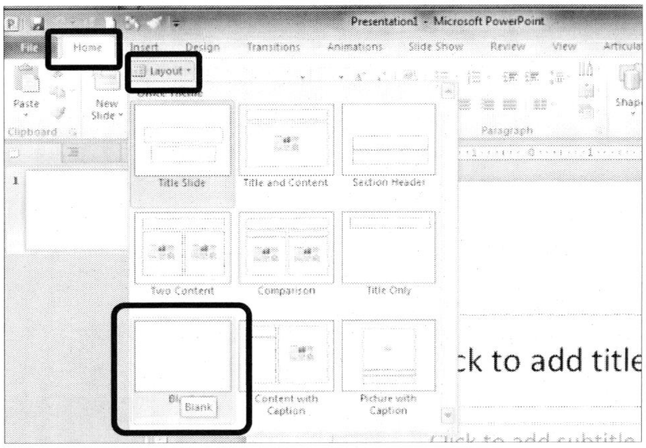

Set the Background Color

1. Right click on the PowerPoint slide.
2. Select **Format Background** from the menu.
3. In the **Format Background dialogue box**, select the type of background you want. For this example, we selected Solid Fill and the Fill color is Black.
4. Click the **Close** button.

   If you have more than one slide, you can clidk the **Apply to All** button to change the background on every slide. With multiple slides, if you select **Close**, it will only apply it to the selected slide.

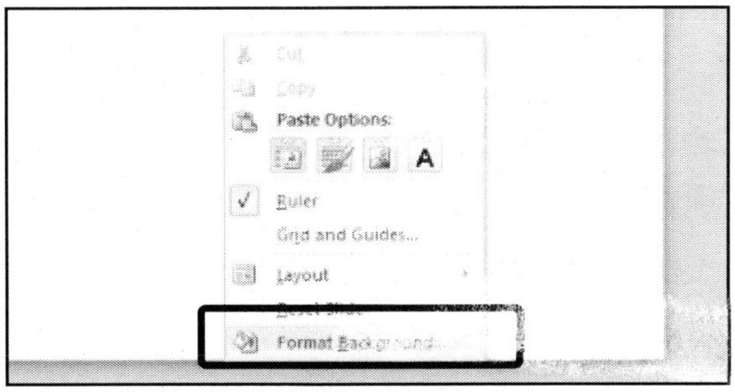

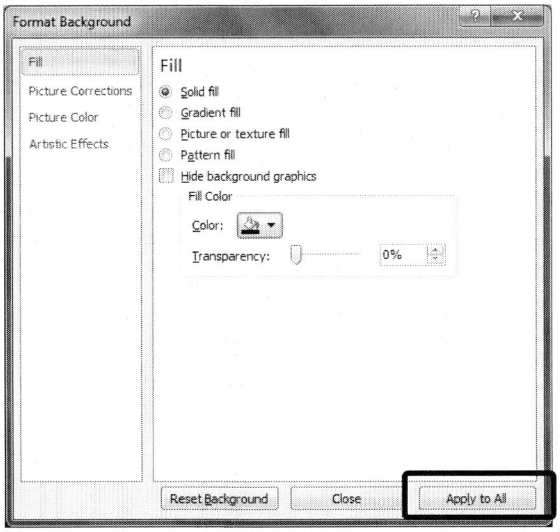

Insert Images onto First Slide

1. Open the **Insert** ribbon.
2. Click the **Picture** button.
3. Locate and select your image (hold the CTRL key as you select if you want to insert more than one).
4. Click the **Insert** button.

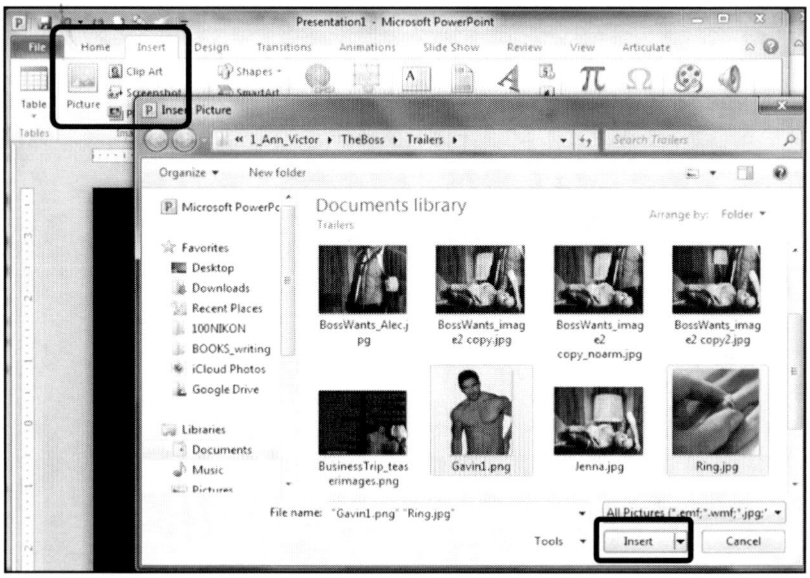

Crop Image

1. Select the image.
2. Open the **Picture Tools Format** ribbon.
3. Click the **Crop** button.
4. Left click and drag the black handles on the image edges to crop.
5. Click away from the image to exit crop mode.

   You can also click the **Crop** button to exit crop mode.

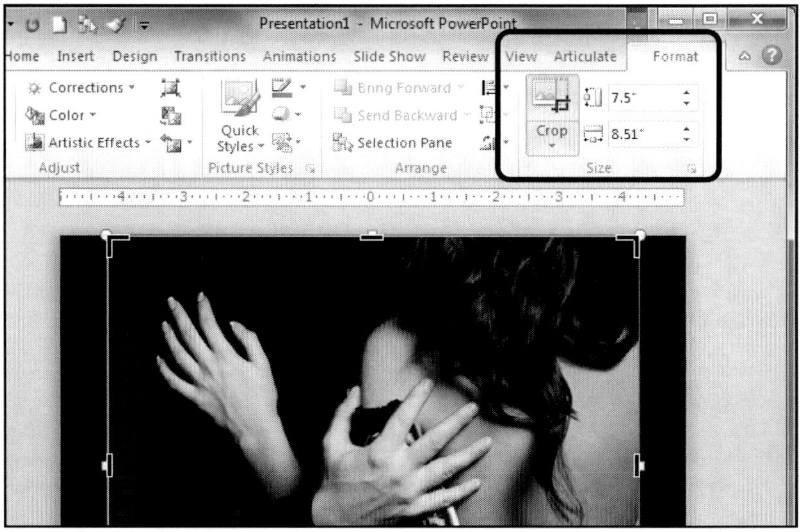

You can also hit **ESC** on your keyboard to exit crop mode.

Resize and Position the Image

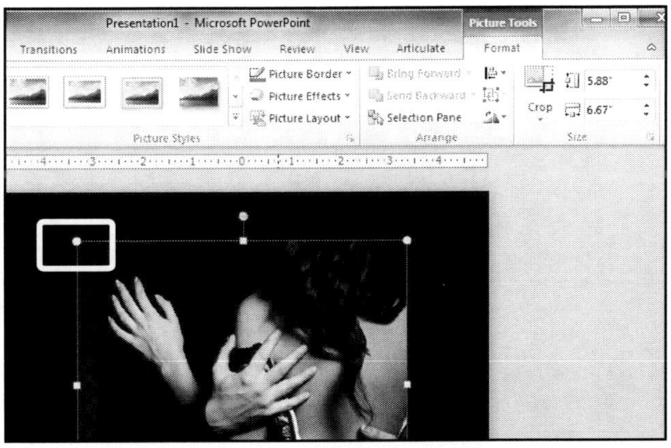

1. To resize: left click and drag any of the 'handles' on the image.

   The round handles at the corners will maintain image proportion/ratio.

   The square handles on the sides and top and bottom will stretch the image.

2. To position: place your mouse over the image – when you see the four-way arrow, left click and drag.

Send Image to the Back

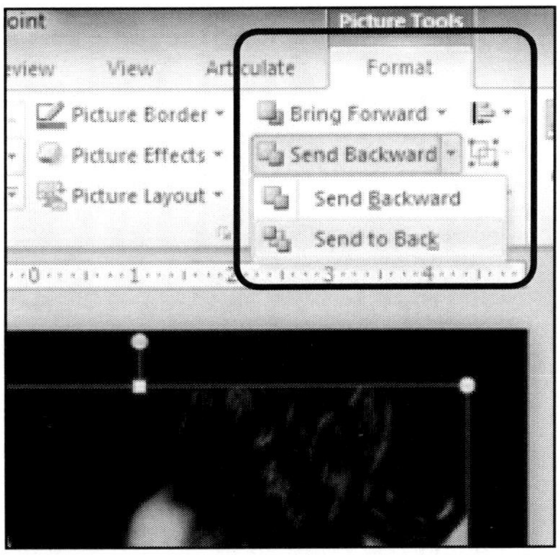

1. With the image selected, open the **Picture Tools Format** ribbon.

2. Click the **Send Backward** down arrow to open the menu.

   If you don't open the menu, the button will send the image backward one layer at a time

3. Select **Send to Back**.

TIP: Use the Selection Pane.

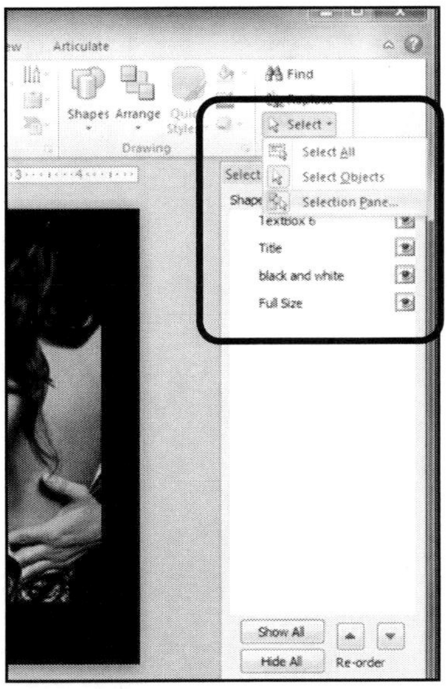

1. From the **Home** ribbon, open the **Select** menu and click **Selection Pane**.

2. You can **hide** images and objects you aren't working with by selecting the eye button to the left of the object.

3. You can **name** your objects by clicking on the existing name and typing a new one. This is really helpful when working with animation.

4. You can **change the layering** (Bring Forward or Send Backward) by selecting an object in the Selection Pane and use the up and down arrows at the bottom of the pane.

Flip an Image

1. With the image selected, open the **Picture Tools Format** ribbon.
2. Click the **Rotate** down arrow to open the menu.
3. Select **Flip Horizontal**.

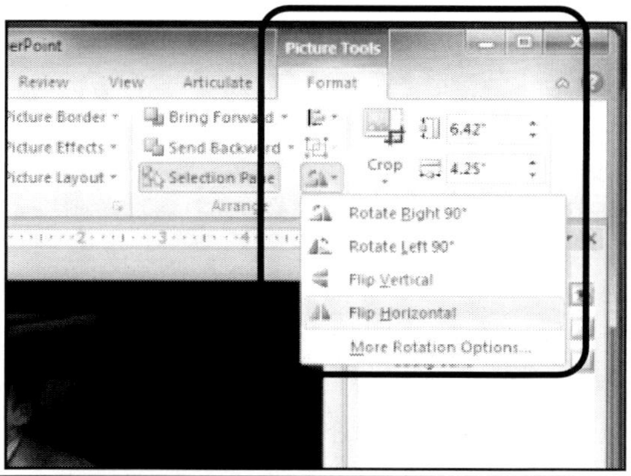

Apply a Picture Style

1. With the image selected, open the **Picture Tools Format** ribbon.
2. Click the **Picture Styles** down arrow to open the menu.
3. Click on one of the styles to apply it to the image.

   If you hover the mouse over a style, the image will preview that style.

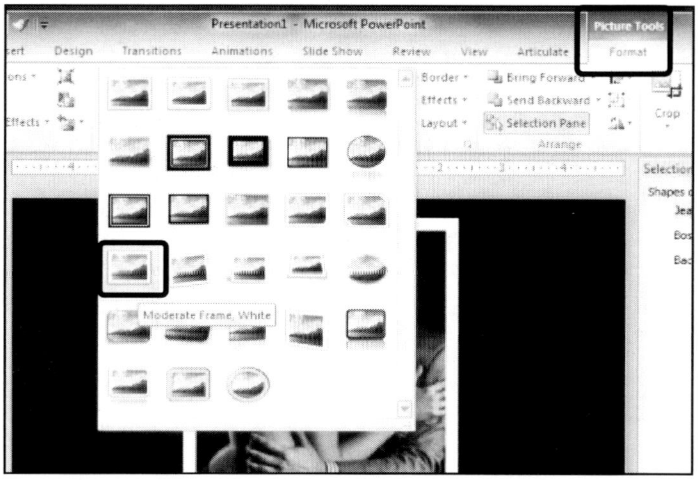

Rotate a Picture

1. With the image selected, grab (left click and hold) the **Green Rotate Handle** and rotate the image to the position you want.

TIP: Use the Format Painter

1. With the image selected, open the **Home** ribbon and click the **Format Painter** button. This will copy the formatting from the selected image.

2. Click on the image to which you want to paste the formatting.

   Only some formats will paste, such as Pictures Styles, Picture Border, Picture Effects, and Color (as well as others). Size, rotation, and cropping are among the formats that will not paste.

Add a Shape

1. Open the **Insert** ribbon and select **Shapes**.
2. Select the shape type you wish to insert.
3. Left click and drag on the screen to draw the shape.
4. You can resize and rotate the shape the same way you do with images.

Apply Color and Transparency to the Shape

1. With the shape selected, open the **Drawing Tools Format** menu.
2. Select the **Shape Fill** down arrow.
3. Select a color from the palette and the color is applied.
4. Alternately, select **More Fill Colors** (as shown here). The **Colors dialogue box** opens.
5. Select the color.
6. Use the slide bar at the bottom to set the transparency.
7. When done, click the **OK** button.

Change the Shape Outline

1. With the shape selected, open the **Drawing Tools Format** menu.
2. Click the **Shape Outline** down arrow to open the menu.
3. Click **No Outline**.
   If you want the shape to have an outline, select the color. Change the thickness using the **Weight** sub-menu and change the style using the **Dashes** sub-menu.

Change the Shape Effects

1. With the shape selected, open the **Drawing Tools Format** menu.
2. Click the **Shape Effects** down arrow to open the menu.
3. Mouse over **Soft Edges** to open the sub-menu.
4. Select one of the soft edge options. When you mouse over one of the options, it will preview on the shape but it doesn't apply the format until you click on it.

Add and Format Text

1. Open the **Insert** ribbon and select **Text Box**.
2. Left click on the slide and type the text. If you left click on the shape, the shape will be converted into a text box. The formats you applied to the shape will remain until you change them.
3. Left click and drag the text to position it on the slide.

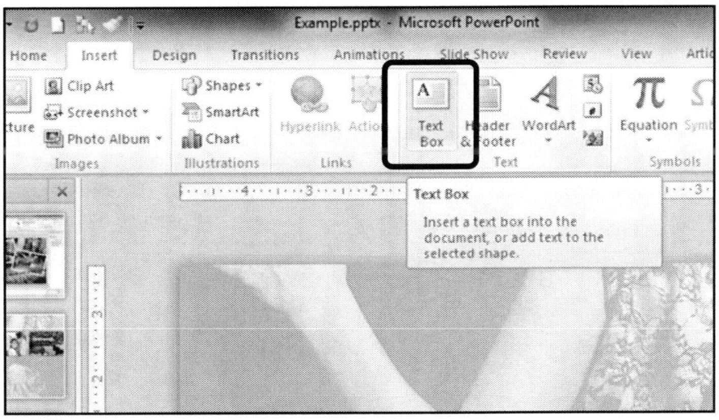

4. Use the **Rotate** handle to rotate the text.
5. From the **Home** ribbon, use the **Font** options to select Font Style, Size, Color, and other font formats.
6. You can also apply formats using the **Drawing Tools Format** ribbon. Play around and get creative. You can always use the Undo button (CTRL + Z on the keyboard) to undo any actions.

Add Image to Master Slide

1. If you are going to use an image that already exists in the presentation, select that image and click the **Copy** button on the **Home** ribbon (or use CTRL+C on the keyboard). If you are going to insert a new image, skip step 1.
2. Open the **View** ribbon and select **Slide Master**.
3. Click on the **Master Slide** with the number 1 beside it.
4. Use the **Paste** button to paste the image (or use CRTL+V on the keyboard).
5. If you are going to insert the image, open the **Insert** ribbon and select the **Picture** button, then locate and select the image.
6. You can apply formatting to the image.
7. When complete, from the **Slide Master** ribbon, click the **Close Master View** button.

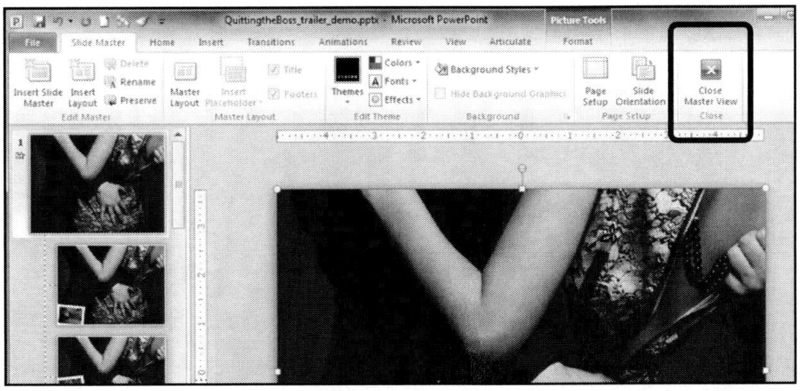

Apply a Color Format to an Image

1. With the image selected, open the **Picture Tools Format** ribbon.
2. Click the **Color** down arrow to open the menu.
3. Select one of the color options (image will preview when you hover the mouse over an option..

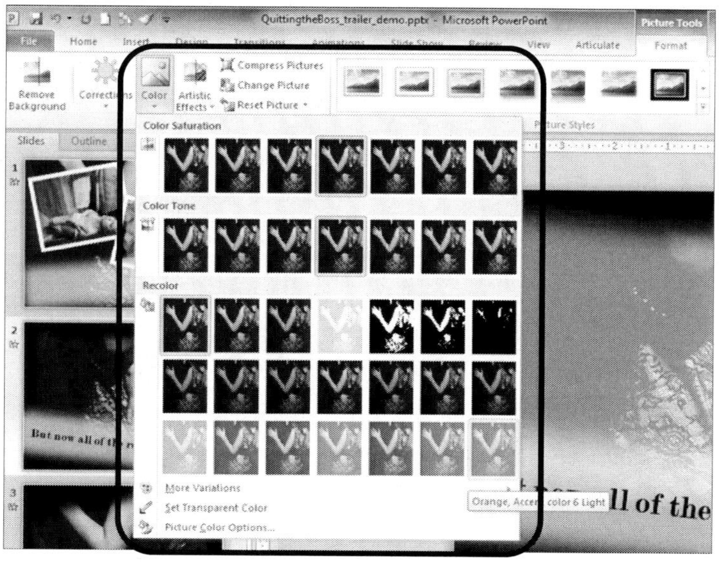

Add Music

1. Open the **Insert** ribbon and select the **Audio** down arrow.
2. Click **Audio from file...**
3. Locate the music file and select it.
4. Click the **Insert** button.

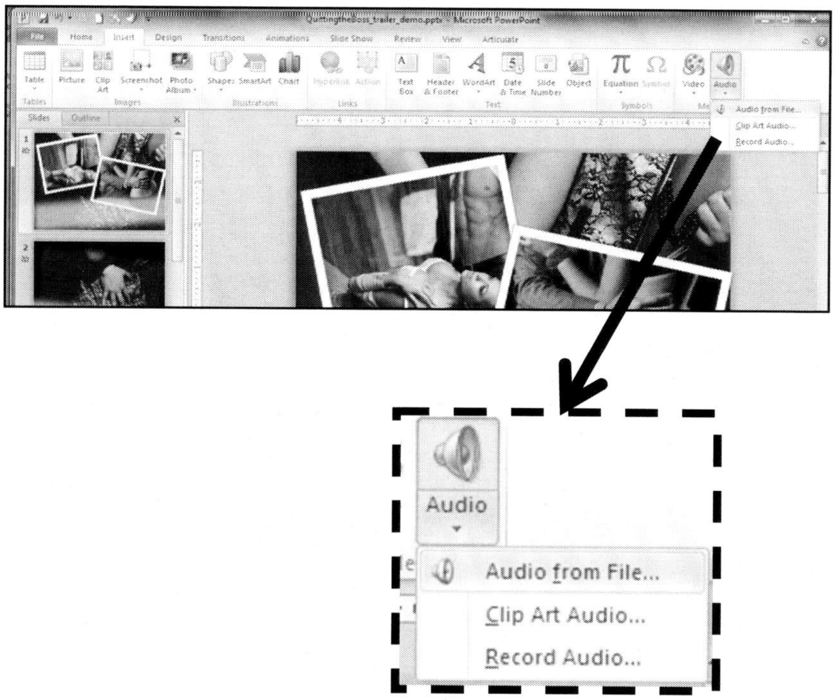

Adjust Music Playback Settings

1. With the Audio file icon selected, open the **Audio Tools Playback** ribbon.
2. For **Start**: select **Automatically**.
3. To have the music to play across all the slides (for the entire trailer), select **Play across slides** for the Start option (you must select **Automatically** first).
4. Click the **Hide During Show** check box so the icon won't appear on the slides.

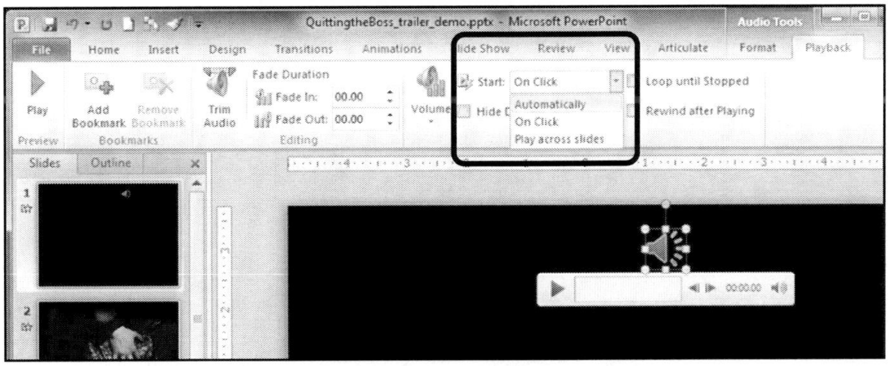

Adjust Music Duration

1. With the Audio file icon selected, open the **Audio Tools Playback** ribbon.
2. Select **Trim Audio**.
3. Left click and drag the green bar to adjust the start time.
4. Left click and drag the red bar to adjust the end time.
5. Click the **OK** button when all edits are complete.

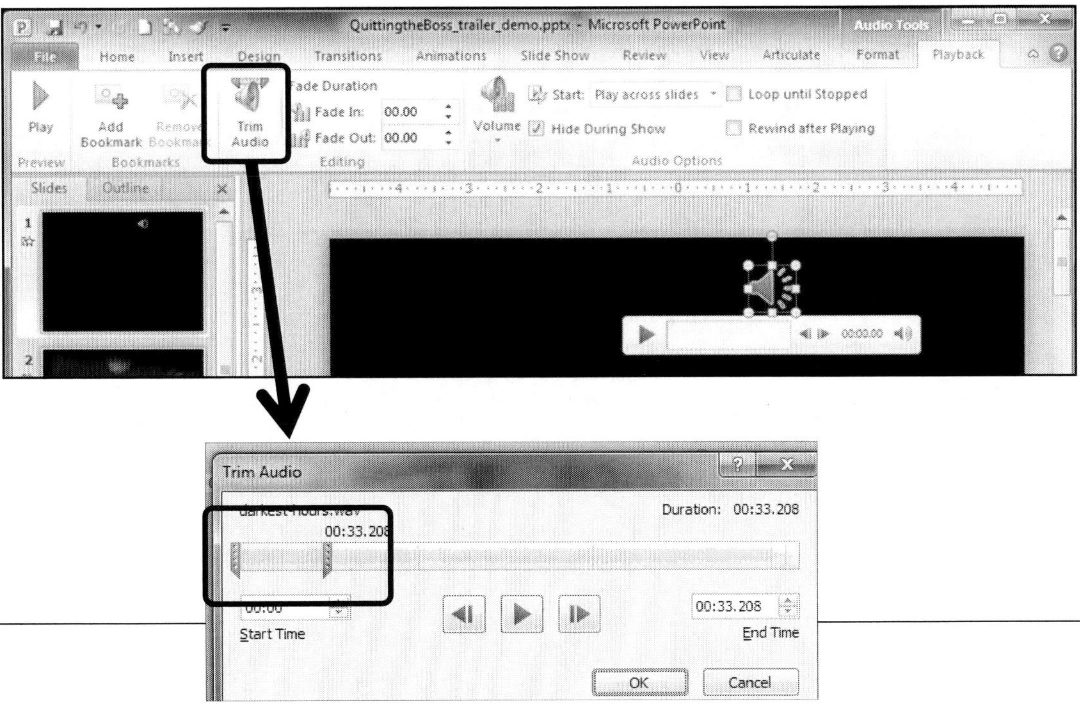

Add Animation

1. Select the image(s) to apply the animation to (to select multiple images, left click on one, then hold the CTRL key as you select the others).
2. Open the **Animations** ribbon.
3. Select the appropriate Entrance, Emphasis, or Exit animation from the options.

Adjust Animation Timing

1. With the animated image (or other object) selected, open the **Animations** ribbon.
2. Adjust the **Start** to using the drop-down menu.
3. Adjust the **Duration** as appropriate (slower or longer) using the up and down arrows.
4. Adjust the **Delay** as appropriate using the up and down arrows.

TIP: It is often easier to work with animations when you have the Animation Pane(shown) open. The button is on the **Animations** ribbon.

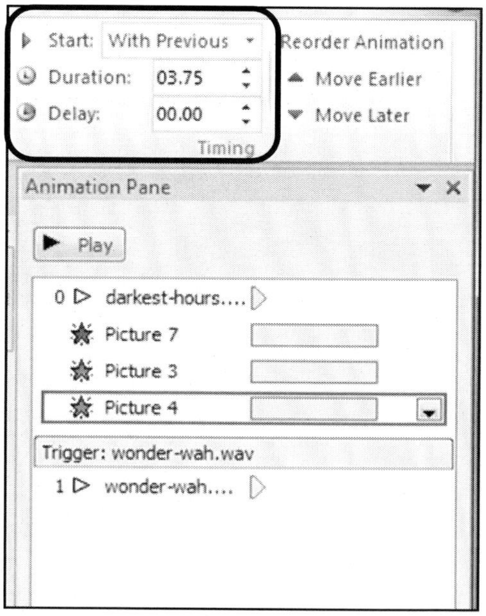

Apply Slide Transition and Adjust Timing

1. Select a transition option from the **Transition**s ribbon.

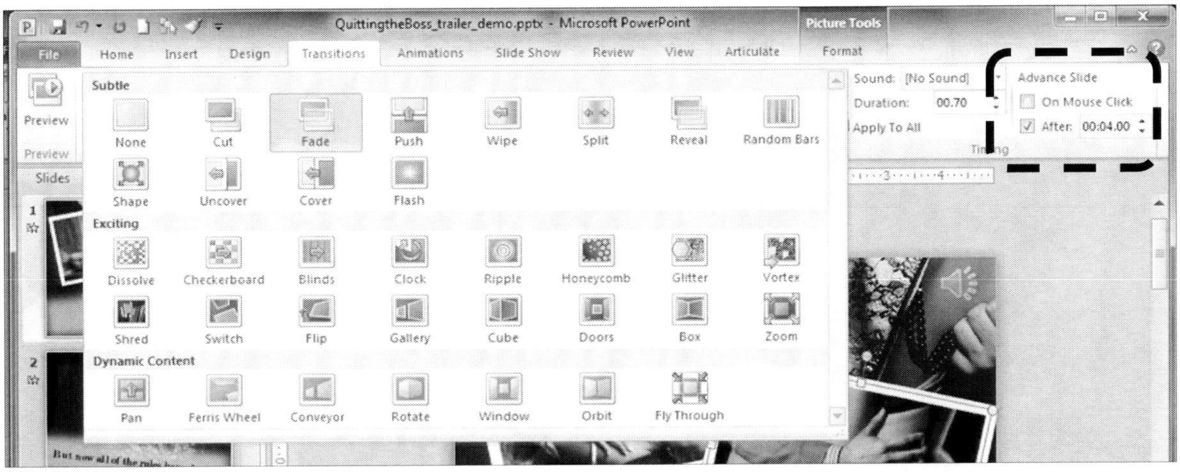

2. Adjust the timing of the transition by selecting the **After** check box and adjusting the time. De-select the **On Mouse Click** check box.

TIP: Select and adjust transitions after all of the slides are created.

Repeat the steps until all slides are complete.

Tips:

- The F5 key will start your slide show from the beginning in PowerPoint.
- Shift + F5 will start the slide show from the slide you are viewing, but if you have music on the first slide that is set to play across all slides, it won't play unless you start from the first slide.
- Add music at the very end and adjust the slide duration/transitions based on the length of the music.

Publish as Video

1. From the **File** menu, select **Save As**.
2. In the **Save as type** drop-down menu, select **Window Media Video (*.wmv).**
3. Give your video a name (it can be the same as the PowerPoint file).
4. Click the **Save** button. It can take several minutes to publish the video. Watch the status bar at the bottom to monitor the progress.

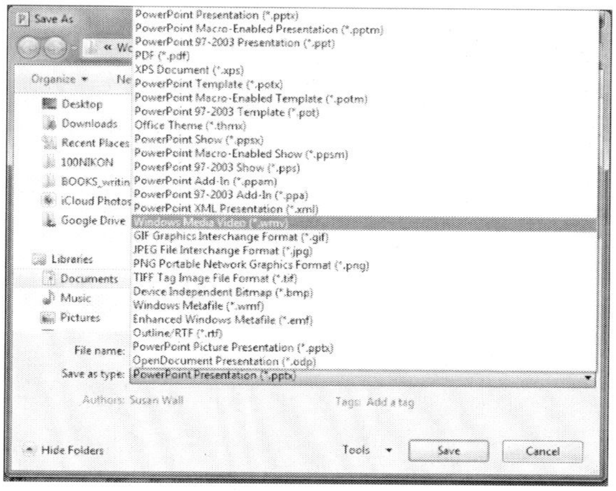

In the folder where you saved the file, the video will have a thumbnail that looks like a filmstrip and the file name will end with .wmv. Double click to open and play the video.

Where to Share Your Trailer

1. Your website.
2. Your YouTube Channel.
3. Facebook.
4. Pinterest.

Appendix A
Standard Photo Release Form

Organization Name:____

____
Address

________________________________ ________ ________________
City State Zip

Permission to Use Photograph

Photo Description:____

Photo Use:____

I grant to *{Insert Organization Name}*, its representatives and employees the right to use the photograph(s) described above in connection with the above-identified Use. I authorize *{Insert Organization Name}*, its assigns and transferees to copyright, use and publish the same in print and/or electronically.

I agree that *{Insert Organization Name}* may use such photograph(s) with or without my name and for any lawful purpose, including such purposes as publicity, illustration, advertising, and Web content.

I have read and understand the above:

Signature ____

Printed Name:____

Organization Name (if applicable):________________________

____
Address

________________________________ ________ ________________
City State Zip

Signature, parent or guardian ______________________________
(if under age 18)

Romance Novels by Susan Ann Wall

A cancer survivor who celebrates in silence…

Aaron Hawkins is a reporter whose assignment is to report on the Relay For Life fundraiser that Hannah Locke's team is holding. But the news report turns into a love story he continues to pursue long after it's gone to press.

A widow who remembers the man she lost…

Hannah Locke has a simple formula for happiness that doesn't include falling in love. Her calculation stops adding up the moment she locks on to Aaron's mesmerizing eyes. Even the memories of the man she vowed to love forever can't keep her heart from learning to love again.

A fight back where two hearts battle to be together…

When Hannah discovers Aaron is a cancer survivor, the heartache of what she already lost have her running from him. Despite her efforts not to love Aaron, their hearts come together to fight back against cancer together.

When cancer threatens everythi8ng, love ignites the flame that burns inside.

Infamous for her blocks on the roller derby circuit, Ballistic Miss L rolls with whatever life hands her. But Malinda Locke's fearless demeanor can't keep her wheels turning when she hears those dreaded three words: you have cancer.

Having lost her brother to cancer, Malinda feels like her family is cursed. She's determined to fight back on her own. Malinda doesn't want her friends and family to suffer the trauma of another battle with cancer. But she soon learns the secret is impossible to keep. Malinda begins to rely on the broody – and sexy- Declan Hall.

As the jammer on the men's roller derby team, he's as fast on eight wheels as he is to come to Malinda's aid. But Declan has three vices. He attends AA to handle his alcoholism and he gnaws spearmint gum to stave the nicotine addiction. But not even the reality of cancer can deter the fixation he has for Malinda.

Coming in 2015!

She promised her husband to keep on living.

He promised his wife to keep on fighting.

Now they will both learn that a second chance at love is worth the fight.

Stacie Nightingale has quit her teaching job mid-year, left her fiancé without a word, and moved across country on an impulse. Even more reckless, the aspiring author has had a one-night stand with a man she doesn't even know...a man she discovers is her new neighbor.

She soon finds herself in a relationship she neither wants nor wants to give up. Like the lingering effects of the car accident that caused her impulsive behavior, Stacie tries to ignore the way he makes her heart race. What she learns is that some things should never be ignored...or kept secret.

Computer security expert Owen Landry has been divorced twice from cheating wives. That alone should make the discharged soldier gun-shy about jumping into a relationship with someone as secretive as Stacie. Owen has always ignored his instincts about women, but this time he's listening to his inner radar. He's ready to leave the past behind and forge a new life...with Stacie. Even though he doesn't like to keep secrets, he's scared his past will make Stacie run. Even if she can look beyond his past, her secrets cause him to question his own heart. Then he realizes she's suffering from post-traumatic stress and a traumatic brain injury that may as well be a ticking bomb. With their future in jeopardy, they find love is the best way to leave the past behind.

Two years ago, Jenny Carter chose her career over the love of her life. Her career is soaring and she's on the cusp of her dream promotion. Jenny's too focused to even realize she's missing a key element in her happily ever after. When her ex-fiancé Ty Sullivan unexpectedly moves to Seattle, shock is soon replaced by suspicion as he steals her client and threatens her promotion. What Jenny can't deny though, is the way the one man she has ever loved still makes her heart race. For a second time, she'll have to decide if her ambitions are more important than her heart. Worse than the ultimatum he delivered in the heat of the moment, Ty regrets not leaving Boston with Jenny Carter. It took him two years, but now that he's in Seattle, he's determined to win her back, no matter what it takes. He's not surprised she's still holding a grudge, but her seething anger has him wondering how he'll ever break through to her passionate heart. When they fall into old habits, he knows they have to break the cycle, but earning her trust could be the biggest challenge he's ever faced.

For Owen Landry, the world is perfect until he asks his girlfriend to move in with him. Shortly after she says no, with no real excuse except that his daughter is coming to visit, his ex-wife shows up at his door and starts doing what she does best - inflicting her poisonous ways on Owen's life. While trying to figure out if the one year old his ex left at his door is actually his son, Owen realizes he can't trust anyone and suspects the secrets Stacie is keeping are one more nail in the coffin of their doomed relationship. He turns to bourbon, his abusive father's answer to the problems that test a man and realizes he's more like the man than he ever wanted to admit. Stacie Nightingale wants to move in with Owen, but ten years with the wrong man has her reluctant to take that next step. She has to get past what she refers to as her Armageddon day, the day she was supposed to marry her ex and what would have been the biggest mistake of her life. While the looming date has her distracted, she knows when it passes, so will her feelings of dread and self-doubt. She doesn't want to hurt Owen, but he knows her too well to let her distractions just fade with the twilight. His ex-wife's timing couldn't be worse, and Stacie is forced to face her own demons in order to help Owen fight his.

It's the best arrangement possible: a friends-with-benefits relationship with the man she's had a crush on for over a decade. Morgan Landry's commitment to her career, coupled with her goal of NEVER being like her mother is what has her going back to Bryan Curtis for more and more...and well, even more. The biggest challenge is keeping it from their coupled-up friends, including her overprotective brother, who are all on the road to marriage, the one destination Morgan has no intention of reaching. When the arrangement sprouts some complications and Morgan starts failing tests and running away from her job, she does her best to deny the true beat in her heart.

Chief Petty Officer Bryan Curtis is married to the navy. He's seen too many marriages fail because of the demands of the military to crave that kind of commitment. Because he likes women, his shallow reputation of pursing blondes has earned him the title of man-whore, a moniker he's never minded until he crosses the line with Morgan. His loyalty to Morgan's older brother – Bryan's best friend – continues to eat away at him, but not enough for him to walk away from the women he's craved for over a decade. Bryan keeps the secret to keep her in his bed, but when his heart gets involved, he has to own up to his feelings and hope it doesn't ruin his friendship with his best friend or have Morgan jumping ship.

Coming soon!

Owen Landry plans to propose to his girlfriend Stacie Nightingale, but waiting for the perfect moment causes circumstances to further delay his plans. Lost memories from Stacie's past reveal a betrayal she can hardly fathom, igniting her own reservations about a future with Owen.

Find out what's coming next by following Susan online:

www.susanannwall.com

www.facebook.com/susanannwall.author

twitter.com/@susanannwall

www.goodreads.com/susanannwall

www.pinterest.com/susanannwall

EROTIC FICTION BY ANN VICTOR

Alec Winter thrives on control, but Jenna Craven has always known the truth about her boss. Finding themselves alone after a work-related gathering at a hotel bar, Jenna's teasing puts Alec's self-control to the test. When they have a repeat performance of what Jenna thought was a one-time thing, they push each other's limits in an erotic game that neither can control.

Jenna Craven has always liked to challenge her boss's steeled self-control, but when he ended their affair two months ago, she stopped playing the game with him. Now Alec Winter doesn't like the idea that Jenna has someone new in her life. He'll risk everything to keep her away from the new guy, and get her back into his bed.

When Jenna Craven started sleeping with her boss, it was simply to push his limits and find some pleasure for herself. Now she's finding she wants more. Knowing that can't happen while he's her boss, she accepts a position in a different department at Logicesse Software. As the Director of Training, she'll report to a different vice-president, allowing her to deal with the circumstances, good or bad, of her proposition to Alec.

Find out what's coming next by following Ann Victor online:

www.annvictor.com

www.facebook.com/annvictorauthor

twitter.com/@annvictor

Made in United States
North Haven, CT
12 November 2026

22222924R00022